NYSTCE SCHOOL BUILDING LEADER 107-108 EXAM

"You never fail until you stop trying" - Albert Einstein

For inquiries;
info@xmprep.com

NYSTCE SCHOOL BUILDING LEADER 107-108 EXAM #1

Test Taking Tips

☐ Take a deep breath and relax

☐ Read directions carefully

☐ Read the questions thoroughly

☐ Make sure you understand what is being asked

☐ Go over all of the choices before you answer

☐ Paraphrase the question

☐ Eliminate the options you know are wrong

☐ Check your work

☐ Think positively and do your best

Table of Contents

TEST DIRECTION

Read the questions carefully and then choose the ONE best answer to each question.

Be sure to allocate your time carefully so you are able to complete the entire test within the testing session. You may go back and review your answers at any time.

You may use any available space in your test booklet for scratch work.

Questions in this booklet are not actual test questions but they are the samples for commonly asked questions.

This test aims to cover all topics which may appear on the actual test. However some topics may not be covered.

Studying this booklet will be preparing you for the actual test. It will not guarantee improving your test score but it will help you pass your exam on the first attempt.

Some useful tips for answering multiple choice questions;

- Start with the questions that you can easily answer.

- Underline the keywords in the question.

- Be sure to read all the choices given.

- Watch for keywords such as NOT, always, only, all, never, completely.

- Do not forget to answer every question.

Students with disabilities are entitled to an appropriate classroom assignment. Which primary legal consideration supports this entitlement?

A) Written requests of parents for placing their children to a particular program or teacher should be granted.

B) Students should have direct access to a trained specialist in their areas of need.

C) Students with disabilities should be placed in learning environments that have special education professionals' supports.

D) It is the right of the students to be educated with nondisabled peers.

A principal is assigned to a school with a history of poor student achievement and decides to address this problem by encouraging the development of a professional learning community within the school. The principal can evaluate the success of this effort by reflecting on the extent of which of the following?

A) The teachers' expressed goals for their development reflect high standards of practice

B) The teachers' mastery of the content of their subject area(s) has increased

C) The teachers are using inquiry and collaboration to improve their practice

D) The teachers show a willingness to expand their use of research-based instructional strategies

The principal of a school assigns teachers to different established teams for them to achieve its fundamental goal, which is to "set and achieve high academic and behavior expectations for every student". These teams also provide several types of professional support to the teachers.

Which of the following questions must the team members focus on addressing to ensure the principle that they are striving to meet their goal?

A) How should we respond when we encounter students who have difficulties in learning?

B) What are the most important skills and lessons for our students to learn?

C) How can we ensure fair application of behavior management approaches?

D) How do our students' lives outside of school impact their performance?

Which of the following strategies must a principal use to ensure that the recommendation of the non-renewal of a teacher's contract due to inadequate performance over a prolonged period would lead to the action he or she desires?

A) Maintain careful documentation of the teacher's poor performance as well as the efforts made by the school to improve said teacher's performance

B) Include with the recommendation the incidents and events that represent the teacher's inadequacies

C) Solicit support from the school staff who share the principal's concern about the teacher's performance

D) Show how the behavior exhibited by the teacher can affect students by citing published educational research

5

Ms. White, an art teacher, collaborates with her colleagues across subject areas and different grade levels to develop an art curriculum that will enhance student learning.

What will this collaboration most probably affect on students' art learning?

A) Students will deepen their appreciation of the importance of peer learning in completing art projects.

B) Students will quickly master artistic skills and techniques.

C) Students will appreciate their teacher's extra efforts spent on improving their art class.

D) Students will acquire more in-depth and broader necessary knowledge to understand art lessons and activities.

6

Which of the following actions must be taken by the principal to facilitate best the acceptance of the teachers to a new student information system on campus that the principal has piloted?

A) Allow teachers to practice using the system before it goes live

B) Allow teachers to do collaborative experimentation for them to learn from each other

C) Arrange for teachers to trained by the system's vendors

D) Highlight how the system will also benefit the teachers' practice

7

For what primary purpose does the Average Daily Membership (ADM) record of every school serve?

A) To document the teacher-student ratios

B) To determine the state funding level received by each school

C) To support the educational accountability of every school

D) To evaluate the trends in school attendance

8

With which of the following is the process of developing unique ideas associated?

A) Creative thinking

B) Critical thinking

C) Reflective thinking

D) Associative thinking

4

A high school has been ignoring the "no pass, no play" policy for several years. As the new school principal, Mr. David wanted to enforce the strict implementation of such plan and wanted to address the issue at an upcoming meeting with the school council.

Which role should Mr. David observe during the deliberation of the issue with the school council?

A) Build internal support from the several council members through discussing with each of them his position privately

B) Present fairly the pros and cons of the strict implementation of the policy

C) Allow each council member to reflect on and evaluate the school's educational mission

D) Offer favors to the council members so that they will support his vision

Which of the following responses should the school leadership institute first cope with the increasing diversity of the student population concerning factors such as students' home languages and cultural backgrounds?

A) Create instructional groupings that would place students with commonalities together.

B) Create a unit of instruction that focuses on multicultural themes.

C) Create an assessment of the capability of the current support systems to meet the needs of the new students.

D) Create exemption from challenging courses to allow students to have successful academic experiences

Which of the following signs should a high school principal most likely observe if there is a possibility of unequal treatment of students in the school?

A) Required classes tend to have twice as many students as elective classes in science and social studies

B) Content-area teachers are delivering the same instructions to all students instead of modifying them for English Language Learners.

C) Participation in fine arts classes by many of the African American, American Indian, and Hispanic students

D) Special needs students attending general classes throughout the entire school day while others visit a resource room for part of the day

After reviewing the results of school culture and climate survey answered by the students, the principal of a school finds unusually low ratings in the section of the study which addresses students' motivation to achieve high marks in academic performance.

Which of the following actions would be the best follow up on this result?

A) Compare students' perceptions with actual performance trends by analyzing students' grades and test scores

B) Try to gain additional insight into the low ratings by increasing informal observation of student interactions

C) Determine whether teachers' ratings show a similar pattern to those of the students by administering a same survey to the teachers

D) Solicit input from the school staff about the likely reasons for low student ratings and the possible solutions

13

Which of the following is the principal's best first step for increasing the energy efficiency of a building with high heating and cooling costs that was built in the 1960s?

A) Encourage the use of fans and space heaters in the classrooms

B) Ask for a list of areas of greatest energy loss in the school from the custodial staff

C) Recommend that the school undergoes a comprehensive energy audit

D) Replace all incandescent lighting with fluorescent lighting

14

A new principal does a time audit for one week by briefly describing her activities, both planned (e.g. meetings, teacher observations) and unplanned (e.g. phone calls from parents/guardians).

What will the principal be able to accomplish by doing this type of action?

A) Identify the barriers in her ability to implement high-priority leadership tasks.

B) Recognize the most crucial components of her daily routine for successful school leadership.

C) Gather concrete evidence for evaluating her current leadership approach.

D) Define the leadership tasks she could do most easily and effectively and delegate to others in the school.

15

The new principal of a school wishes to build the school's capacity for distributed leadership despite being a school that used the top-down management approach. The principal can initiate efforts to achieve this goal by providing teachers and other members of the staff with opportunities that will enable them to demonstrate and enhance their ability to do which of the following?

A) Attain specified aims by directing the efforts of others

B) Create various plans that are in line with the school's vision and goals

C) Collaborate with colleagues and other school stakeholders

D) Adhere to different school protocols, schedules, and deadlines

16

Why is it essential for a speaker to make eye contact with members of the audience?

A) It tells the audience that he is confident in the material.

B) It tells the audience that he is dishonest.

C) It creates a bond of distrust.

D) It makes the audience less likely to remain engaged.

A principal of an elementary school that has a good performance record believes that teaching and learning in the school could be improved. Thus he decides to promote this improvement by creating a school environment that encourages innovation and responsible risk-taking among its faculty members.

Which of the following strategies would most likely contribute to the development of this type of situation?

A) Implement a system that regularly updates the faculty on current trends and research in elementary school education

B) Provide the faculty with regular opportunities for collaborative problem solving and sustained support for implementing workable solutions

C) Provide considerable autonomy to the faculty by allowing them to select student learning goals and to determine how to achieve them in their classes

D) Visit classrooms regularly and offer the faculty praise for what they are doing well as well as provide suggestions for addressing some observed needs

Which approach out of the following has been known to give the most effective results when it comes to increasing group productivity?

A) Select a bigger team, since the pool of ideas would, therefore, be more significant.

B) Swap roles between members, therefore a supervisor wouldn't be the one always to make the last decision.

C) Select a diverse team regarding gender, ethnicity, age, and work experience.

D) Select members that together form an equilibrium of the criteria of the HBDI (Herrmann Brain Dominance Instrument) system.

19

A middle school principal asks teachers during a faculty meeting to generate a list of strategies that they can use in their classes to remedy the problem involving students coming from diverse cultural backgrounds who are not fully benefitting from the instruction they receive in class.

Which of the following suggestions would be the most appropriate to find on the list?

A) Allow students some flexibility in defining their own learning goals and determine how to achieve them

B) Divide students into groups based on previous performance and implement varied curricula to these different groups based on their strengths and needs

C) Use examples that are most likely to be familiar to all students to illustrate and clarify instructional content

D) Focus on basic knowledge and gradually incorporate higher-level learning after the students master the basic concepts

20

How could a press release be best used to communicate about a school decision?

A) Through it, the school principal can establish a system of awards for recognizing student achievements.

B) Through it, the school principal can grant permission to homeschool other students.

C) Through it, the school principal can transfer substantial funds from one budget account to another.

D) Through it, the school principal can change the school's guidelines regarding behaviors.

21

Which of the following reasons is the most important for maintaining a database of building maintenance and repair records of a specific school?

A) To identify approved vendors when purchases are required

B) To promote effective organizational management

C) To prevent emergency repairs from occurring within the facility

D) To encourage the school staff to have a more efficient energy consumption

22

Which of the following actions represents a consistent and acceptable school accounting procedure?

A) Receipts for purchasing school decorations for a school dance are submitted, and expenses are deducted from ticket sales.

B) A teacher asked for reimbursement upon presenting a receipt of a high-quality used computer for the school resource room.

C) An account is established to handle the small everyday school expenditures such as postage stamps.

D) The ticket sales of a school concert were deposited in the music director's checking account and then gives a check with the total amount received by the school.

23

A principal appoints a committee of language arts teachers to investigate potential writing programs for the school after agreeing with the site council that the school should focus on writing improvement during the next three years. In reviewing the committee's proposal, the principal realizes that the new program will need substantial changes in instructional practices for many teachers.

Which of the following steps would be most useful for the principal to take to make the transition to the new program smooth?

A) Request that teachers submit a weekly progress report to document their implementation of the new program.

B) Arrange for teachers to visit and observe classrooms in other schools that have already implemented the new program.

C) Develop a plan for providing teachers with ongoing professional development during the implementation of the new program.

D) Have the committee develop a series of short-term goals for teachers to achieve during the implementation of the new program.

24

A rural school seeks to increase its access to technological resources for teaching and learning. However, the school is significantly experiencing funding problems.

Which action should the school administrators do to achieve this goal?

A) Collaborate with educators from the more affluent and technologically advanced schools to learn various strategies.

B) Seek support from local businesses that may have interest in having partnerships in achieving the school's goal.

C) Cut other areas of the school's budget plan and use it to increase the technology funding.

D) Solicit for public assistance in raising funds for the school through publicizing its needs in newspapers and other local media.

25

Which of the following steps should school principals take first to build a budget after the central office informs them to expect a 20% cut in the operating budget of their respective campuses?

A) Cut all budget lines by the same amount to maintain equality among all programs

B) Provide the campus improvement committee with budget lines that are essential to the schools' operation

C) Share the information with the faculty and staff and tell them about the areas to be cut so they can anticipate reductions

D) Notify the campus improvement committee of the programs and services that will be cut based on the reduction

26

Which of the following is not considered as a use of standardized assessments?

A) To evaluate whether students have learned what they are expected to learn

B) To determine whether educational policies are working as intended

C) To identify gaps in student learning and academic progress

D) To use standardized test results to alter classroom curriculum

27

Curriculum guides are documents used by states, school districts and individual schools to guide teachers in their instruction. Many guides are detailed, giving teachers a specific scope of what to teach and when. Many provide additional resources, such as necessary materials and assessment tools.

Which of the following about curriculum guides is not correct?

A) It can be based on the grade level of students.

B) It helps teachers decide what to teach and when

C) It can not be based on the number of students in each class.

D) It helps teachers decide on classroom management strategies.

28

Which of the following is not correct about communication?

A) Nonverbal communication is the use of body movements to send a message.

B) If a speaker uses graphs, charts he is using an assertion of logic.

C) It is never appropriate to use obscene language in a speech.

D) Pitch has a psychological effect that influences how people perceive your speech's content.

29

Which of the following terms is not defined correctly?

A) Development is the continuous process of change that all humans experience during their life.

B) Learning is the change of behaviors, thoughts or emotions based on genetics.

C) Growth is the physical process of development.

D) Maturation is the physical, emotional or intellectual process of development.

30

To abide by new state requirements, the Assistant Superintendent (ASP) plans to revise the high school social studies curriculum, especially since the members of its department have always had different opinions about it. What would be considered a right approach for the ASP to take?

A) Convene a meeting with the social studies department to explain the new state requirements and ask for their opinion on how to best meet them.

B) Convene a meeting with the department and suggest revisions.

C) Ask members of the department to help in revising the curriculum.

D) Ask the department of social studies to revise the curriculum themselves.

31

A school's current 10-year old vision has not been used in a significant way for many years. Thus, the school principal decides to initiate a process of developing a new vision.

In what way can the creation of the new vision most benefit the school?

A) Ensuring accountability for results

B) Achieving positive school change through reducing potential barriers

C) Providing a clear sense of direction where the school should move forward

D) Aligning curriculum, instructions, and assessment

32

What should teachers keep in mind when designing instruction?

A) Not all kids are on the same level.

B) Instructional planning isn't as crucial as it's believed.

C) All students understand the same way.

D) The previous experiences of students aren't the base of learning.

33

Which of the following defines the role of a teacher in a student-centered environment?

A) Law enforcer who makes sure students are following the rules and regulations.

B) Co-teacher who works alongside the students to deliver lessons.

C) The organizer who monitors and supports student activities.

D) The dictator who tells students what to do and controls all their actions.

34

During the process of improving some aspects of campus operations based on campus goals, an elementary school teacher used a variety of strategies, such as establishing an advisory committee, surveying parents and teachers for their input, and holding public meetings to answer questions on proposed changes to help him lead the initiative to this goal.

Which of the following is right about the principal in this given situation?

A) The principal is using the strategies primarily to promote a sense of ownership for any implemented changes.

B) The principal is using the strategies primarily to ensure that stakeholders respect each other's perspectives.

C) The principal is using the strategies primarily to avoid and eliminate disagreements amount stakeholders that involve the proposed changes.

D) The principal is using the strategies primarily to ensure that the necessary changes will reflect the will of the majority of the school community

Which of the following actions must a middle school principal do to help the site-based decision-making (SBDM) committee move forward in selecting a new health education curriculum when some of its members express their dissatisfaction with some aspects of the new curriculum implemented in the school?

A) Suggest that the committee explore more different curricula and select the one they want implementing

B) Ask the team to reexamine the aspects of the curriculum they have chosen that are causing dissatisfaction

C) Remind the team that going backward in the task assigned to them would possibly affect their milestone dates

D) Meet with team members individually to gauge their position on the chosen new curriculum

A school team will be developing the school's emergency response plan to promote awareness and educate the school community about what to do in case of a natural disaster or a human-caused emergency situation. Which of the following would be the first step in forming such a plan?

A) Research relevant laws and regulations to help strengthen the school's emergency response plan

B) Meet with community leaders to assist the school in various worst-case scenarios

C) Solicit information from public health, fire, and local police personnel about appropriate responses to vulnerabilities

D) Benchmark with the emergency plans of other schools across the state

37

Mrs. Fowler, a middle school principal, would like to seek the broader participation of diverse stakeholders in crafting the school plan.

What should Mrs. Fowler primarily do as the initial step to achieve this goal?

A) Join in a district committee to create districtwide policies promoting diversity awareness.

B) Create a committee of diverse stakeholders and empower them to recommend strategies to be included in the school plan.

C) Seek support from the president of the school's parent organization to recruit advisory group members.

D) Publish in the school newsletter the importance of a broader stakeholders' participation in school governance.

38

Which of the following actions should a school principal take to make school safety a priority after reading an article written by a local newspaper reporter who easily gained entry into the school through an unlocked side door?

A) Determining whether additional security cameras can be purchased by reviewing the campus budget

B) Requesting a meeting with the superintendent to ask for funds to hire security officers

C) Reminding everyone in the school community on each morning announcement that unidentified visitors should be reported to the office

D) Reviewing procedures for securing the building by meeting with the custodial, office, and teaching staff

A school principal wants to create a team to plan and design a program for improving mathematics achievements of the students. The team was at first considering to include the principal, an assistant principal, teacher representatives per grade level, and the district math coordinator. Later, it was decided to add representative parents in the team. What would be the most critical benefit of including parent-representatives in the team?

A) It expands the range of perspectives and ideas that will contribute to the problem-solving process.

B) It recognizes various school constituents as contributors to solutions on education issues.

C) It encourages the development of a more positive, balanced, and productive team.

D) It promotes a broader communication with the school community the school's commitment to improving math performance

Jane is the principal at a junior high school that receives Title I funds. One of the teachers comes up to her and angrily tells her that one of her colleagues, Mr. Miller, comes into her class and takes up half of her course with their teaching on a daily basis. She requests something to be done about this. Mr. Miller is a title I teacher, so Jane assures the teacher that she will take care of the issue that same day.

Which of the following is the best course of action for Jane in dealing with Mr. Miller?

A) Inform Mr. Miller that his role as a title I teacher does not allow him to take up half the class' time for instruction.

B) Ask Mr. Miller to discuss this matter with the teacher to avoid future problems.

C) Place Mr. Miller on the corrective action because he is not abiding by his job's description.

D) Write up an incident report on the conflict between the teachers.

41

A high school's site-based decision-making (SBDM) committee has developed four options for a new open-campus policy that they have been considering that allows its student to eat lunch off campus. The options range from the current closed-campus policy to an open-campus policy.

Which of the following would be the best next step in the decision-making process?

A) Decide on one option that you wish to build support for in the school community by voting amongst themselves

B) Allow students to voice their support for the option they prefer by holding assemblies

C) Determine which best satisfy the campus' needs and preferences by conducting a pilot test for each option

D) Gather information about the benefits and drawbacks of each plan from schools with different open-campus plans

42

A school district's school board has collaborated with the community, the police and the local judicial system to come up with a search policy that will help guide the school officials when performing searches of the students' lockers, their backpacks, and the school grounds. This policy also includes urine drug tests and body searches in case some students engage in activities that don't comply with school rules or incidents that can lead to safety risks happen.

Which of the following is a crucial element for the school board when it comes to search the policies?

A) The date when there is a change in of the school policy.

B) The expected result for all types of school searches.

C) The ability to share with the media the outcomes of the school searches.

D) The mission statement the school policy.

During an observation of a mathematics lesson by a high school principal, he sees that a teacher uses an online simulation focused on changing geometric shapes as a teaching tool. The students use this online simulation to make hypotheses about the forms and discuss them with a partner in an online forum.

Which of the following is the primary purpose of the teacher for using this teaching technique?

A) Reinforce routines also processes

B) Establish workplace readiness

C) Develop critical-thinking skills

D) Sustain student interest

Significant disparities in the kindergartners' literacy backgrounds have been noted in a particular district, in which some pupils are proficient readers while others have no prior reading experiences.

What must educators do to best ensure that an equal opportunity is given to all young children to become successful readers?

A) Providing an early intervention program which pupils and their parents can openly participate

B) Encouraging collaboration between kindergarten teachers and reading specialists for reading classes

C) Providing computer-based literacy programs in kindergarten classrooms

D) Creating an extended time for reading instruction for targeted pupils

SECTION 1

#	Answer	Topic	Subtopic	#	Answer	Topic	Subtopic	#	Answer	Topic	Subtopic	#	Answer	Topic	Subtopic
1	D	TA	SA1	12	D	TB	SB2	23	C	TA	SA1	34	A	TB	SB2
2	C	TA	SA1	13	C	TB	SB1	24	B	TB	SB2	35	B	TA	SA1
3	A	TA	SA2	14	A	TB	SB1	25	B	TB	SB2	36	C	TB	SB2
4	A	TB	SB2	15	C	TB	SB1	26	D	TA	SA1	37	B	TA	SA1
5	D	TA	SA1	16	A	TB	SB1	27	D	TA	SA1	38	D	TB	SB2
6	D	TB	SB2	17	B	TA	SA2	28	D	TB	SB1	39	A	TA	SA2
7	B	TB	SB2	18	D	TB	SB1	29	B	TA	SA1	40	A	TB	SB2
8	A	TA	SA2	19	C	TA	SA1	30	A	TA	SA1	41	D	TA	SA2
9	C	TB	SB2	20	A	TB	SB2	31	C	TA	SA2	42	D	TB	SB2
10	C	TB	SB2	21	B	TB	SB1	32	A	TA	SA1	43	C	TA	SA1
11	B	TA	SA2	22	C	TB	SB2	33	C	TA	SA1	44	A	TA	SA2

Topics & Subtopics

Code	Description	Code	Description
SA1	Instructional Leadership	SB2	Operational Management
SA2	Visionary Leadership	TA	Leadership
SB1	Organizational Management	TB	Management

CONTINUE ▶

TEST DIRECTION

DIRECTIONS

Read the questions carefully and then choose the ONE best answer to each question.

Be sure to allocate your time carefully so you are able to complete the entire test within the testing session. You may go back and review your answers at any time.

You may use any available space in your test booklet for scratch work.

Questions in this booklet are not actual test questions but they are the samples for commonly asked questions.

This test aims to cover all topics which may appear on the actual test. However some topics may not be covered.

Studying this booklet will be preparing you for the actual test. It will not guarantee improving your test score but it will help you pass your exam on the first attempt.

Some useful tips for answering multiple choice questions;

- Start with the questions that you can easily answer.

- Underline the keywords in the question.

- Be sure to read all the choices given.

- Watch for keywords such as NOT, always, only, all, never, completely.

- Do not forget to answer every question.

1

A student with cerebral palsy finishes an assignment. While watching him, an elementary art teacher notices that the student is having difficulty using certain art materials.

Which of the following is the most appropriate for the teacher to address special needs of this student?

A) Providing the student with a range of material alternatives

B) Sharing observations with the student's occupational therapist

C) Assigning the student a different art project

D) To find materials the student can easily manipulate

2

Which factor has been most responsible for decisions to place greater emphasis on developing students' problem-solving and decision-making skills across the curriculum?

A) The increasing influence of media in teaching and learning

B) The change in occupational demands in both local and global societies

C) The increase in educational accountability of every school

D) The change in inclusion practices in every school

3

To ensure the creation of a new and efficient student code of conduct for a school or district, which of the following guidelines must be applied?

A) Behavior expectations and consequences for infractions must be described as precisely, comprehensively, and concretely as possible.

B) Define appropriate behavior expectations and consequences included in the code using the school's or district's vision.

C) Define behavior expectations and consequences for infractions so that it will be possible to accommodate substantial flexibility and judgment in enforcing the code.

D) Emphasize behavior expectations and consequences for infractions that reflect the students' experiences in their homes and community

Mrs. Stanley, a school guidance counselor, proposed to implement an innovative guidance program that has been proven successful in other schools. If you were the school principal, what should you do first before deciding on the proposal?

A) Determine whether or not the proposed program will cost more than the allotted school guidance program budget.

B) Evaluate the possible effects of the proposed program in the professional development of the guidance staff.

C) Evaluate whether the proposed program's goals and activities are consistent with the vision and objectives of the school.

D) Determine whether the proposed program will provide opportunities for broader collaborations among the school's staff.

5

A teacher has implemented learning objectives for a unit of study. Which of the following steps should the teacher take next?

A) Put in order the activities to help students meet the learning objectives

B) Implement strategies for presenting concepts related to the learning objectives

C) Identify skills that students will need to develop in meeting the learning objectives

D) Determine how to evaluate students' mastery of the learning objectives

A type of testing, that regularly assesses students for systematic change or improvement, is called as;

A) Achievement test

B) Internal testing

C) Interim assessment

D) Dynamic assessment

7

A teacher's performance is evaluated annually using a teacher evaluation system which uses student performance on standardized tests as a criterion for judging. Which of the following is most important for school-level administrators to take into consideration when implementing the system effectively and equitably?

A) The difficulty level of the standardized test(s) taken by each teacher's students
B) Number of students in the class(es) that each teacher is assigned to teach
C) Test scores achieved by each teacher's students in previous years
D) Scope and challenge of the curriculum each teacher is teaching

8

Which of the following would be the best assistance to the school to become a resource for the community?

A) Parent resource center
B) School newsletters
C) Parent-teacher conferences
D) All of the above

9

In defining goals for a professional growth plan for a new teacher, which of the following factors should play the greatest role?

A) Annual school and district priorities for improvement
B) Results of observations of the teacher's performance
C) Types of development resources and support available for the teacher
D) Teacher self-evaluation of needs in relation to state and district standards

CONTINUE ▶

A school's mission statement emphasizes the role of the school in "enabling students to become confident, self-directed, lifelong learners" and "preparing students to participate actively as responsible citizens in an ever-changing society."

In what way can the school principal facilitate the achievement of the goals in the mission statement?

A) Guide the stakeholders to define a set of specific, concrete objectives aimed at accomplishing each goal.

B) Guide the stakeholders to enumerate assessment procedures for measuring students' current performance about each goal.

C) Guide the stakeholders to determine the resources and materials required for each goal.

D) Guide the stakeholders to determine strategies for addressing each goal in various content areas.

The primary goal of a school's new principal is to ensure continuous academic improvement for all students despite having a poor academic performance for some student groups as well as high rates of teacher turnover. Which of the following information must the principal find in order to best achieve this goal?

A) Ways to improve job satisfaction for high-performing teachers and those with strong potential

B) Workable strategies for increasing teacher autonomy in the classroom while still maintaining a focus on vision achievement

C) The extent to which teachers have a voice in determining the courses and students they are assigned to teach

D) Current teacher pay and benefits at the school in relation to pay and benefits in neighboring schools and districts

A new principal in a low-performing school was met with resistance from teachers when he suggests eliminating some instructional practices that they use and replaces them with methods that have been proven more effective in promoting student learning. The principal finds research that indicates that the teachers' readiness to learn and change teaching styles partly depends on their confidence and self-esteem. Which of the following approaches can the principal use to motivate his teachers after the information he has found?

A) Have the teachers assess their own needs and draw their conclusions about how to improve their performance using new teaching practices.

B) Introduce new teaching practices to teachers through the use of low-risk activities in small-group settings.

C) Ask the teachers to research on targeted new teaching practices before asking them to try the methods themselves.

D) Create a list of new teaching practices for the teachers to incorporate independently into their teaching at their own pace.

A principal organizes a committee of teachers, specialists, parents/guardians, and community members to help develop a plan to improve the school's integration of technology into instruction, but after a few meetings the committee had little progress and they have started to lose interest.

Which of the following ways effectively help the principal to motivate the committee members to put in the time and effort that is necessary to ensure the success of the plan?

A) By establishing a rotating chair to ensure that each committee member is responsible for conducting one or more meetings

B) By reminding committee members that they willingly agreed to serve on the committee and are jointly responsible for its success.

C) By identifying manageable, short-term goals and tasks and giving each committee member a responsibility for achieving a specific goal or task

D) By asking each committee member to develop and present to the rest of the group a set of recommendations about what to include in a plan

14

Which of the following gives some ways to improve students' reading, writing, listening and speaking skills?

A) Asking questions and criticizing students work

B) Listening to the students

C) Encouraging discussion

D) None of the above

15

A vision statement is a school's roadmap, indicating both what the school wants to become and guiding transformational initiatives by setting a defined direction for the school's growth.

What does an effective vision statement focus on?

A) Promotion of community diversity

B) Teamwork between teachers and students

C) Continuous professional development of the school's teachers and other staff

D) High expectations for student learning

16

Critical thinking is a disciplined thinking that is clear, rational, open-minded, and informed by evidence.

Which of the following is recommended during the critical thinking process?

A) Considering the consequences of your conclusion

B) Avoiding discussing the origins of your point of view

C) Avoiding focusing on statistical evidence since most people care more about personal stories

D) Judging all points of view as equally valid and acceptable

17

What are the advantages of Sean's old and worn school being refurbished over the course of the summer vacation going to be, other than enhancing its general appeal?

A) Teacher improvement

B) Student improvement

C) Teacher and student improvement

D) None of the above

18

In Ms. Murray's English class, the students were asked to predict the outcome of a story. The students were given one minute to think of their predictions before they have been invited to share with a partner their ideas. Some students then voluntarily describe to the whole class their predictions.

Which instructional strategy was used in the situation?

A) The anticipation guide strategy

B) The reciprocal teaching strategy

C) The shared reading strategy

D) The think-pair-share strategy

19

A school where assessment is not currently used as a driving tool for instruction hires a new principal who has a goal of creating an effective, data-driven instructional program. Which of the following questions would be the most important one for the new principal to address first to achieve their goal?

A) What types of existing achievement issues at this school are best addressed through data analysis?

B) How can enough time for collaborative data analysis and discussion be built into teachers' schedules?

C) In determining when and how to use data analysis to plan instruction, how much flexibility should teachers have?

D) What is the most efficient way to involve a broad cross-section of school stakeholders in data analysis activities?

Which of the following should the principal do first to address the concerns of parents/guardians regarding teachers in the upper elementary grades not assigning their children with enough meaningful homework?

A) Encourage teachers to provide students with more challenging homework assignments by meeting them individually.

B) Recommend the development of homework guidelines for each grade to be made by the collaboration of both site council and faculty and staff.

C) Create a committee of teachers, parents/guardians, and staff who would study the homework issue and make recommendations about it.

D) Suggest that the parent/guardian organization present a prepared report on the homework issue in the upcoming faculty meeting.

A majority of fourth graders at an elementary school were found to score far below the standards in math on the most recent statewide assessment. The same majority of fourth graders were found to score a level approaching the standards in reading and writing. Which of the following steps should the school staff find most useful to take first in analyzing these results?

A) Determine whether the problems are system-wide by comparing the fourth-grade test data with other elementary schools within the school district

B) Find out whether there have been significant changes in the performance of this group of students by reviewing third-grade test data from the previous year

C) Compare the fourth-grade test data with the report card grades received by the school's fourth graders during the school year

D) Determine the performance and needs of specific student groups by disaggregating the test data for the entire school

Which of the following practices is the least efficient way for a school leader to build staff morale?

A) Striving to provide resources a teacher requests

B) Recognizing teachers publicly for their exemplary performance

C) Relieving teachers of the pressure of making leadership decisions

D) Involving teachers in planning and evaluating school activities

By adopting the Common Core Standards, a school most directly reflects the state's commitment to:

A) ensuring accountability for teachers, schools, and districts

B) guaranteeing that graduates have the knowledge and skills needed for college or career success

C) delivering culturally responsive instructions and address the students' diverse needs

D) strengthening collaboration with other states to improve learning achievement

CONTINUE ▶

24

A principal will be leading a team in updating the school's old emergency response plan so that members of the school community will know what to do in case of a natural disaster or a human-caused emergency situation. Which of the following steps would be most useful to take first in this effort?

A) Meeting with community leaders to identify individuals and resources available to assist the school in various worst-case scenarios

B) Reviewing the emergency plans of a sample of similar schools across the state and comparing them with the school's current plan

C) Soliciting information from local police, fire, and public health personnel about potential school vulnerabilities and appropriate responses

D) Researching each element of the school's current emergency plan to assess compliance with relevant laws and regulations

25

Which type of performance assessment lets the teacher decide what the students are able to do for long periods of time?

A) Extended performance assessment

B) Individual performance assessment

C) Restricted-response performance assessment

D) Authentic performance assessment

26

School principals of a district recognize the need of providing schools with ample hardware, software, and teacher training to promote students' learning. However, there is fund inadequacy for supporting such need.

What should the principals primarily do to gain access to needed financial resources?

A) Ask funding supports from foundations and grants

B) Ask the support of local government officials through parents' solicitations

C) Publicize the initiative through local media to gather funding supports

D) Seek funding from the district's state representative

27

In her walkthroughs, Bellamy notices that certain students have some concerning coping abilities and she brings it to the attention of other teachers. They decide to involve the community and let the parents know in order to come up with different solutions and ideas together. What is the actual purpose behind this?

A) Adhere to state regulation

B) Collaborate with the community

C) Address the issues

D) Involve non-instructive staff

28

A school principal decided to initiate a review of the school maintenance practices due to many complaints about them.

Which approach should the school principal take in initiating this review to make it most cost-effective and least disruptive?

A) Spending money on arising repair issues only and completing each repair efficiently

B) Making and observing preventive maintenance activities schedule

C) Doing significant repairs at the end of the school year and minor maintenance as soon as possible

D) Conducting inspection and maintenance system at the end of every semester

29

Which of the following is the most appropriate initial response a high school principal must have when the parents of a student who receives special education services due to his disability threaten to file a complaint with the Office for Civil Rights if the school does not put their son on the basketball team?

A) Allow the student another try out with his parents present

B) Direct the parents to the basketball coach for an assessment of their son's basketball skills

C) Ask for advice from the district's Title IX coordinator regarding the legal aspects of the situation

D) Explain the laws that relate to students with disabilities and the selection criteria for competitive programs

30

Which of the following about basic terms of development is not correct?

A) Nurture refers to the effect of the environment upon a person.

B) Nature refers to the traits that are inherited.

C) Maturation is limitless but Growth is limited.

D) Learning new skills is an example of growth.

31

A disagreement between five council members, with three of them agreeing on one view while the other two expressing their opposition to a specific school issue has already become an impasse.

What must the school principal best do to achieve consensus among the council members?

A) Point out the essential ideas about the opposing views and use them to make an alternative option.

B) Support the majority view and dismiss the minority's ideas.

C) Be neutral on facilitating the discussion while encouraging both groups to identify common ground.

D) Clarify to both groups that the decision should be in the best interest of the school.

32

Which of the following defines validity best?

A) The degree to which an assessment tool produces stable and consistent results

B) The extent to which a test accurately measures what it is supposed to measure

C) The extent to which an assessment measures the achievement of desired objectives

D) The extent to which an assessment covers all the items that have been taught or studied

CONTINUE ▶

A school has significantly increased student enrollment, resulting in a need for more instructional space. As a response to the problem, some space currently used for noninstructional activities will have to be turned into regular classroom space.

In making such response, which of the following should the school principal do first?

A) Seek the approval of appropriate district staff before reassigning any instructional space within the building

B) Ensure that any changes in space utilization will not impair the achievement of the school's vision and goals

C) Select the space changes only to those that cause the least amount of disruption

D) Gather ideas from the parents regarding the issue of space changes

A school's student newspaper editorial members received feedback from a prominent municipal leader about their being highly critical and personally offensive editorials to local officials. Consequently, the school principal was notified to enforce limits on the types of articles published in the school newspaper.

What should the principal respond to this issue?

A) Establish guidelines for the content of editorials.

B) Explain to the municipal leader that students' freedom of expression cannot be restricted unless it poses a substantial risk of disrupting the learning process.

C) Tell the municipal leader to discuss the concerns to the district governing board.

D) Offer the municipal leader a schedule to discuss the concern with the school council.

A new principal of an elementary school with low student achievement records wants to encourage the teaching staff to engage in the process of instructional improvement so that the academic success of the school will raise? Which of the following would be the most appropriate first step to achieve this goal?

A) Meet informally with the teachers and remind them of the importance of participating in efforts to improve instruction in the school

B) Arrange to provide financial incentives for teachers who plan and implement changes in their instructional programs that will help meet their goal

C) Analyze student performance data with the school teachers to help them identify instructional areas that should be modified and improved

D) Ask teachers to monitor campus goals for instructional improvement and the criteria for evaluating whether the goals have been achieved

Which of the following is not a correct definition?

A) Metacognition means thinking and learning about one's own thinking and learning processes.

B) The schema is a term used by Piaget referring to a mental construct that one forms to understand the environment.

C) Assimilation happens when the existing schema needs to be modified to take in new information.

D) Self-efficacy is a term used by Bandura for self-confidence in one's ability to complete a specific task.

The schema is an abstract concept in cognitive development, which was first used by Piaget. He emphasized the importance of schemas and described how they were developed or acquired.

Which of the following defines schema best?

A) It is a cognitive framework or concept that helps organize and interpret information.

B) It defines the process of saving knowledge in the brain.

C) It refers to the first phase of cognitive development.

D) It is a term used to explain how the brain develops.

Which of the following about assessment is not true?

A) The most significant quality of a good assessment is validity.

B) An assessment is the process of gathering and discussing information from multiple sources to develop a deep understanding of what students know, understand, and can do with their knowledge as a result of their educational experiences.

C) A standardized test is any form of test that requires all test takers to answer the same questions or a selection of questions from a common bank of questions.

D) While interpreting raw scores, knowledge of basic statistics is essential.

39

Cognitive development is the construction of thought processes, including remembering, problem-solving, and decision-making from childhood through adolescence to adulthood.

Which of the following about cognitive development is not correct?

A) Knowing the number of days in a year is an example of crystallized intelligence.

B) Memory loss and Dementia is a symptom of Alzheimer's disease.

C) Remembering a password to enter into a website is an example of using short-term memory.

D) An individual's attention span typically decreases through adolescence and childhood.

40

Freud (1905) proposed that psychological development in childhood takes place in a series of fixed stages.

According to Freud's Psychosexual Development Theory, which of the following stages is associated with elementary school ages?

A) The Latency stage
B) The Genital stage
C) The Oral stage
D) The Phallic stage

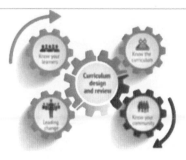

Curriculum design is a statement which identifies the elements of the curriculum, shows what their relationships are to each other. It also indicates the principles and the requirements of organization for the administrative conditions under which it is to operate.

Which of the following about curriculum design is not correct?

A) The curriculum is a material that teachers teach.

B) Curriculum models provide a framework for curriculum guides.

C) Backward design in curriculum planning is designing the end of the day before designing the beginning of the day.

D) Curriculum planning helps make sure teaching on a daily basis has a larger purpose.

Which of the following about sensory and perceptional development is not correct?

A) Sensory perception is defined as the change in sensation that we experience with age.

B) The categories of sensitive periods are; language, order, sensory skills, motor skills and social skills.

C) The term "sensitive periods" is associated with Maria Montesorri and Hugo de Vries.

D) A condition where a person receives little or no sensory input is called as sensory deprivation.

43

Teachers are discussing the importance of following the principles created under the Code of Ethics for Educators. The first principle discussed is Principle 1, which states that the educator will accept responsibility for which of the following?

A) Teaching students that they can act in whatever way they please.

B) Resting all ethical responsibility on the principal

C) Teaching students that they should not have character traits

D) All of the above

44

Vygotsky is an educational psychologist who is well known for his sociocultural theory. According to this theory, social interaction leads to continuous step-by-step changes in children's thought and behavior that can vary greatly from culture to culture.

Which of the following about cognitive development and Vygotsky's theory is not correct?

A) Vygotsky used a sociocultural perspective in his theory of cognitive development.

B) Staying cognitively active is helpful for maintaining both fluid and crystallized intelligence.

C) According to Vygotsky, scaffolding is the process of constructing an internal representation of external physical objects or actions.

D) Lev Vygotsky is most well-known for a cultural-historical theory of cognitive development emphasizing social interactions and culture.

SECTION 2

#	Answer	Topic	Subtopic	#	Answer	Topic	Subtopic	#	Answer	Topic	Subtopic	#	Answer	Topic	Subtopic
1	B	TA	SA1	12	B	TB	SB2	23	B	TA	SA2	34	B	TB	SB1
2	B	TA	SA1	13	C	TA	SA1	24	C	TB	SB2	35	C	TA	SA1
3	A	TA	SA2	14	A	TA	SA1	25	A	TA	SA1	36	C	TA	SA2
4	C	TA	SA2	15	D	TA	SA2	26	A	TA	SA2	37	A	TA	SA1
5	C	TA	SA1	16	C	TB	SB1	27	B	TA	SA1	38	D	TA	SA1
6	D	TA	SA1	17	C	TB	SB2	28	B	TB	SB2	39	D	TA	SA1
7	C	TA	SA1	18	D	TA	SA1	29	D	TB	SB2	40	A	TA	SA1
8	A	TA	SA2	19	B	TA	SA1	30	D	TA	SA2	41	C	TA	SA1
9	B	TA	SA1	20	C	TB	SB1	31	C	TB	SB1	42	A	TA	SA1
10	A	TB	SB1	21	B	TA	SA1	32	B	TA	SA1	43	D	TA	SA2
11	A	TA	SA1	22	C	TB	SB2	33	B	TA	SA1	44	C	TA	SA1

Topics & Subtopics

Code	Description	Code	Description
SA1	Instructional Leadership	SB2	Operational Management
SA2	Visionary Leadership	TA	Leadership
SB1	Organizational Management	TB	Management

CONTINUE ▶

TEST DIRECTION

DIRECTIONS

Read the questions carefully and then choose the ONE best answer to each question.

Be sure to allocate your time carefully so you are able to complete the entire test within the testing session. You may go back and review your answers at any time.

You may use any available space in your test booklet for scratch work.

Questions in this booklet are not actual test questions but they are the samples for commonly asked questions.

This test aims to cover all topics which may appear on the actual test. However some topics may not be covered.

Studying this booklet will be preparing you for the actual test. It will not guarantee improving your test score but it will help you pass your exam on the first attempt.

Some useful tips for answering multiple choice questions;

- Start with the questions that you can easily answer.

- Underline the keywords in the question.

- Be sure to read all the choices given.

- Watch for keywords such as NOT, always, only, all, never, completely.

- Do not forget to answer every question.

CONTINUE ▶

1

According to Hunter, there are seven elements crucial to effective instruction. In which element would modeling be included?

A) Instruction
B) Anticipatory effect
C) Additional reinforcement
D) Guided practice

2

Which of the following is the effect of a hierarchical communication in which a principal first tells the information to the department chairs, then, has been relayed to grade-level team leaders and lastly to team members?

A) Consistent with the principal's intention
B) Inconsistent with the principal's intention
C) Clearer than the principal's intention
D) Higher impact than the principal's intention

3

Which of the following should be the principal's primary concern in evaluating the teachers for the improvement of students' writing scores?

A) If the prepared lessons are based on the teachers' capabilities and mastery
B) If the teachers' lesson match the objectives with the third-grade language-arts standards
C) If the teachers include more complex activities for the students
D) If the teachers match their lesson plans with the lessons they are teaching

4

The previous principal of Gateway Middle School, in order to lessen teacher absenteeism, eliminated the substitute service and required the teachers to call their own subs. Majority of the teachers approached the new principal, Mr. Pablo, to reinstate the sub service.

What information should Mr. Pablo use to decide whether or not to bring the sub service back?

A) Comparison of teacher absenteeism before and after the sub service
B) Test scores of the students
C) Teacher's opinions
D) Discipline rates among students

5

What action should a school building leader take to create collaborative relationships among staff?

A) Encourage out-of-school get-togethers

B) Group employees based on performance and skill

C) Promote respect and effective communication

D) Encourage faculty to resolve problems on their own

6

A school leader should have the ability to select the appropriate data to inform his instructional and curricular decision making. Which of the following information would be most valuable to help a department chair in determining the reason for low test scores of some students in the advanced-physics class?

A) Admission scores of the students in the advanced-physics class

B) Teacher records of tests grades, homework assignments, and class participation

C) The complexity of the lessons taken

D) Comparison of test scores of students from advanced and non-advanced physics class

7

Mr. Zafra is testing whether Ms. Williams, a prospective teacher, could interact professionally with parents. He asks Ms. Williams how she would react if a parent starts an argument at the parking lot.

How should Ms. Williams communicate to the parent?

A) I understand how concerned you are about your child, but I feel that these matters should be discussed privately. When should we schedule our meeting?

B) You have a very unruly child. Please learn how to discipline him so as to avoid humiliation.

C) You should talk to the principal about these matters.

D) Come to the classroom tomorrow, and we will talk.

8

Of the following disciplinary issues, which requires the most care on the part of the school building leader?

A) Truancy

B) Interrupting teachers

C) Dress code

D) Insubordination

9

Seniors at the Glendale High School started a massive food fight. What should the principal do to restore order?

A) Have the teachers stop the riot and the custodians clean the mess up.

B) Let the fight subside and make the students help the custodians with the cleaning up.

C) Close all the doors to the cafeteria and have the teachers clean the food up.

D) Close all the cafeteria doors and have the students clean up the mess, no one leaves until the mess is gone.

10

Standardized tests are administered at the end of the term in order to determine the overall success of instruction. What form of assessment is standardized testing?

A) Summative assessment

B) Formative assessment

C) Continuous assessment

D) Prospective assessment

CONTINUE ▶

11

A school leader should have a great understanding of the steps in the process of addressing an educational problem. Which of the following would help a principal in making a plan to improve third-grade students' scores on the coming state standardized tests for science?

A) Conduct assessment to identify specific areas of weakness in students' performance

B) Review the complexity of the curriculum

C) Extend class hours for science class

D) Collect information about the instructional methods, materials, and assessments currently in use

12

PPBS was a budgeting system developed in the 1940's used to develop the cost of programs.

What does PPBS stand for?

A) Planning Projects Budgeting Service

B) Projects and Programs Budgeting Service

C) Program Projected Budgeting System

D) Planning, Programming, Budgeting System

13

Which of the following should be the teachers' initial step after bringing the compiled copies of students' writing tests to share with the group?

A) Prepare score statistics of all the papers to show frequency of failure marks

B) Identify students that are most needed to improve their writing skills

C) Sort out students with highest test scores to be an example for other students

D) Review all papers to identify common areas of weakness

14

Which of the following will improve when teachers become involved in changes?

A) Culture

B) Camaraderie

C) Morale

D) Test scores

15

Pamela is a school district leader. She sees to it that she attends extracurricular events like scholastic decathlons, debates and science fairs at each school regularly. Which is the most important benefit of this?

A) Giving parents and guardians multiple opportunities to state their concerns to the school district leader

B) Allowing the district leader to be updated about each school

C) Making the district students and staff feel appreciated and supported

D) Setting high expectations for each and every event

16

In recent years, the participation of students in extracurricular activities at the Pawnee Middle School has declined significantly. What step should one initially take to solve this problem?

A) Lessen the number of extracurricular programs

B) Call for parent volunteers

C) Gather information about the decline

D) Give out incentives for participants

17

Mr. Brown is in the process of designing new curricular units to suit his classes better. Which of the following is not considered as a sequential step to designing curricular units?

A) Take note of daily or weekly lessons

B) Collect resource materials

C) Recommend strategies for instruction

D) Carry out daily formal progress checks

18

According to the Occupational Safety and Health Act of 1970, which of the following should the employers make their employees be aware of?

A) Laws regarding wage and hours of job

B) Workplace hazards and health issues encountered on the job

C) Right to have health compensation extending up to a year after job dismissal

D) Requirements for other bonuses and compensation

CONTINUE ▶

The goal of summative assessment is to evaluate student learning at the end of an instructional unit by comparing it against some standard or benchmark. Summative assessments are often high stakes, which means that they have a high point value.

Which of the options given below can be considered as an example of a summative assessment?

A) A standardized state exam

B) Writing a journal

C) A quiz

D) A peer/self-assessment

From 8:00 am to 10:00 am, students at a Montessori school have a Dr. Seuss Pajama Day wherein they dress up in their pajamas while making arts and crafts. This activity requires the participation of two volunteer parents who will each read a Dr. Seuss book. They will also ask the children about the book.

Which of the following is encouraged by this activity?

A) Montessori principles

B) Well-roundedness

C) Reading literacy

D) Community involvement

21

A principal should have the knowledge on developing and monitoring a budget process that involves appropriate stakeholders. Which of the following should a principal do if he observes that the school is not following some district procedures for money management?

A) Scan through the guidelines of money management and give further recommendations to the district.

B) Train all staff on implementing proper accounting controls, procedures, and records for school funds.

C) Hire an accountant to do the money management duties.

D) Let the district personnel handle the situation.

22

A comprehensive database which contains classroom test and quiz scores, formative assessment results, scores from standardized tests, and report card grades for students in each class at each grade level has been created and overseen by a principal and used by teachers to enter new information as well as review existing information.

Which of the following goals would be accomplished effectively by the teachers' use of the database on a regular basis?

A) Strengthening teachers' sense of collective accountability

B) Strengthening teachers' instructional decision making

C) Facilitating ongoing evaluation of grade -level curricula

D) Facilitating increased collaboration between teachers

23

A charter school is a school that receives government funding but operates independently of the established state school system in which it is located, and in some cases is privately owned.

Which of the following should a superintendent do when a dean of a charter school asks if their students can participate in the district's art competition?

A) Refuse the dean's request since competition is not open for charter schools.

B) Refuse the dean's request since there is a difference in the curriculum of charter schools.

C) Grant the dean's request but collect the registration fee.

D) Grant the dean's request since students in charter schools are entitled to participate.

24

A new school district leader told Mr. Jeffreys that he has been having many problems causing him stress. According to him, several other building leaders are under the same pressure. Which strategy should Mr. Jeffreys use to address this issue?

A) He should express gratitude to each building teacher for their hard work.

B) He should regularly check the building leaders individually or via small groups to provide support which could help them reduce stress and solve the problems they are facing.

C) He should limit the working hours of the building leaders.

D) He should encourage the building leaders more to keep their fire burning.

25

Bullying is a distinctive pattern of harming and humiliating others, specifically those who are in some way smaller, weaker, younger or in any way more vulnerable than the bully.

Which of the following should a principal respond to bullying in a school?

A) Inform parents of what the consequences if a child is found guilty of bullying

B) File suspension or expulsion request for students who are guilty of bullying based on the frequency and intensity of bullying

C) Organize a comprehensive anti-bullying program with the support of the community

D) Give additional credits to students who report cases of bullying

26

Which of the following would help a school leader in selecting the most accurate method for evaluating the effectiveness of a course of study in meeting other objectives?

A) Reviewing data that indicates the degree of students' mastery of course objectives

B) Reviewing anecdotal records that describe students' interpersonal growth during the course

C) Conducting surveys for parents to assess the improvement of their children throughout the course

D) Performing students' post-assessment test on all the previous lessons taken

27

Creativity development is a nonlinear and multifaceted process starting early in life. Which of the following about creativity development and intelligence of a child is not correct?

A) Sternberg proposed The Triarchic Theory

B) Child's creativity can be assessed by The Torrance Test

C) Adoption studies show evidence of a genetic influence on intelligence

D) Crystallized intelligence refers to the knowledge that remains stable over the years.

28

Which of the following explains collective bargaining?

A) Negotiating teachers' salaries, benefits, and working conditions with the district administration and the teachers' association

B) Implementing new plans from the head department to each school personnel

C) Ensuring that any legal proceeding is based on established judicial rules, practices, and safeguards

D) All of the above

29

Which of the following would provide objective, quantitative, and specifically targeted data for evaluating school's new science program that aims at enhancing scientific reasoning of students?

A) Providing surveys for students to assess their own performance

B) Setting measurable goals and evaluating student's performance in meeting them

C) Creating test results' comparison for the previous year and present classes

D) Analyzing the performance evaluations of teachers participating in the program

30

It is crucial for a district-level management team to assess stakeholders' views about an issue regarding district schools before they make a decision. This could be done through surveys or interviews. When using the interview approach, which of the following is most likely to be their goal?

A) Gathering information that can be easily interpreted

B) Eliciting detailed responses from stakeholders

C) Minimizing cost with regards to data gathering

D) Making sure that a large representative sample of the stakeholders will participate

31

Which of the following should a school leadership do to foster direct and purposeful involvement of community members in school's mission?

A) Provide each community members of any fund-raising for the school.

B) Inform the community members on activities that need volunteers.

C) Send letters to inform the community members on future plans.

D) Seeking out representative community members to serve on school committees.

32

A test procedure is a standardized and documented process for conducting an evaluation.

During teachers' evaluation of a state exam, they observe the inappropriateness of time distribution to the exam questions. They ask the principal on how to deal with the questions. Which of the following should a principal do in addressing the issue of testing procedures?

A) Teachers must follow the test regulations strictly despite their concerns.

B) Teachers can set their time for the questions.

C) Teachers may not give the state exam while waiting for possible changes.

D) Teachers can give an extension for the overall exam.

33

Excellence is what you strive for when you believe in what you are doing and that the value of what you do warrants the persistent commitment to its betterment.

Which of the following should principal demonstrate to show the best means of communicating a commitment to excellence?

A) Model high expectations for self and others in the school and community

B) Set new high goals to achieve for all the school personnel

C) Create detailed instructions to specify roles of each school personnel

D) Allow school personnel to make their decisions for improvement based on their assessment

34

How can a school district leader promote support for upcoming change initiatives that will affect district schools?

A) By providing a comprehensive data analysis determining the need for change.

B) By interacting face-to-face with interest groups to discuss and understand their concerns.

C) By allowing the media to cover the on-going changes.

D) By constructing plans that would detail how changes would be implemented.

35

The school district leader offered advice to a district governing body on how to deal with a sensitive matter they were discussing. Though some of the members agreed with the school district leader, the majority voted on using a different approach. How should the school district leader respond?

A) Convince the majority to carry on with his own plan

B) Create a compromise solution with those who agreed with him

C) Tell those who agreed with him to support the decision of the majority

D) Support the majority's decision and determine the best way to implement it

36

Three schools from Eagleton are over 50 years old and are in need of renovation. Which of the following is the best initiating action the school district leader can do to approach the problem?

A) He could start a fund-raising activity to collect enough money for building repairs.

B) He could submit a request to the district governing body asking for financial support for a construction proposal.

C) He could arrange for stakeholder groups to tour the new buildings similar to those that need repair.

D) He could instruct the staff to investigate what needs to be done in the buildings.

37

Nowadays, more and more people access content through the internet. This made the district leader consider uploading a letter about expenditure forecast document to a website instead of sending mail through courier. What should the district leader take note of most importantly in considering this option?

A) Members of the intended audience may not have access to the internet to check the website.

B) Members of the intended audience may not trust internet content as much as they do for mail.

C) Information posted on the internet may be modified by unauthorized personnel.

D) Aside from the intended audience, other individuals may also access the letter.

38

Which of the following is the most appropriate action for a high school principal to take when a junior who wants to pursue a career in writing and his parents submit a written request to add a creative writing course as an English department elective in the coming school year?

A) Explain to the parents that study courses are designed to meet general interests of all the students in the school community and not just the special interests of one.

B) Ask members of the English department if they are qualified and willing to teach a creative writing course.

C) Present the parent's request at a closed board of trustees meeting.

D) Ask the curriculum committee to determine if the level of student interest would make it possible to add such a course as an elective

39

A school department chair must have knowledge of how state standards are used to measure the quality and appropriateness of a curriculum.

Which of the following should a new department chair's initial step in evaluating a nine-year curriculum that the teachers said to be outdated?

A) Collaborate with the teachers to examine the alignment between the existing curriculum and observe classroom instruction

B) Consult with the board of education for further instructions

C) Prepare survey forms for the students and parents about their insights about the curriculum

D) Study research programs for high school English curriculum

40

A professional learning community, or PLC, is a group of educators that meets regularly, shares expertise, and works collaboratively to improve teaching skills and the academic performance of students.

Which of the following would best help a principal in allocating funds to support the growth of the school's newly established professional learning communities (PLCs)?

A) Provide bonuses for teachers that allow their time in meeting their PLCs

B) Assign new personnel to handle PLCs and give higher compensation

C) Pay for training for the teacher leaders who facilitate and oversee the work of the PLCs

D) Purchase a commercial program that focuses on inquiry-based learning

41

The Individuals with Disabilities Education Improvement Act states that schools are required to provide "free appropriate public education" to children with disabilities. What is the meaning of this statement?

A) Every eligible student with an identified disability must be provided special education services that surpass an array of services for his disability.

B) Every eligible student with an identified disability must be provided with an Individualized Education Program tailored to his special needs.

C) Every eligible student with an identified disability must be provided an Individualized Education Program enabling him to achieve his maximum potential.

D) Every eligible student with an identified disability must be provided the same education as any public school student.

42

Which of the following is most essential to a school district's educational vision?

A) Guiding district improvement through constant communication to create a clear image of the future of the community based on the community's own insights

B) Providing a roadmap to achieving the district's goals and expectations

C) Gaining the support of the public via defining the primary functions of the school district

D) Setting expectations with regards to the nature and extent of collaboration among community members

43

A school head should have the knowledge of the basic due process protections afforded to school personnel. Which of the following is guaranteed to all school's personnel under the constitution and key court rulings?

A) Exemption for disciplinary action based on good performance level shown in work

B) Presence of a defense counsel at any hearing and the right to fuse to testify

C) Adequate notice of the charges against them and a hearing in which they have the opportunity to defend themselves against those charges

D) Right to have any number of witness's statement and assure their credibilities disregarding any background

Aria, the principal of Lagoon Middle School has safety issues regarding the bus lanes during dismissal. Sports practices and other extracurricular activities leave him understaffed at the end of the day. Besides this, one of his assistant principals is also ineffective and frequently absent.

If Aria needs another adult to monitor the students boarding the bus, what should she do?

A) Ask the coach to start practice a little later than normal so he could help with the bus lanes.

B) Talk to the assistant professor about his absenteeism and about plans to change this.

C) Ask another teacher who is working in the cafeteria to help with the bus lanes.

D) Change the students' dismissal times so as to prevent too many children from occupying the bus lanes.

SECTION 3

#	Answer	Topic	Subtopic	#	Answer	Topic	Subtopic	#	Answer	Topic	Subtopic	#	Answer	Topic	Subtopic
1	A	TA	SA1	12	D	TB	SB2	23	D	TA	SA2	34	B	TB	SB1
2	B	TA	SA2	13	D	TA	SA1	24	B	TB	SB1	35	D	TB	SB1
3	B	TA	SA1	14	C	TA	SA2	25	C	TB	SB2	36	D	TB	SB1
4	A	TB	SB2	15	C	TB	SB1	26	A	TA	SA1	37	A	TB	SB1
5	C	TB	SB1	16	C	TA	SA1	27	D	TA	SA1	38	D	TA	SA2
6	B	TA	SA1	17	D	TA	SA1	28	A	TB	SB1	39	A	TA	SA1
7	A	TB	SB2	18	B	TB	SB1	29	B	TA	SA1	40	C	TA	SA2
8	C	TB	SB1	19	A	TA	SA1	30	B	TB	SB1	41	B	TB	SB2
9	D	TB	SB2	20	C	TB	SB2	31	D	TA	SA2	42	A	TA	SA2
10	A	TA	SA1	21	B	TB	SB1	32	A	TA	SA1	43	C	TB	SB1
11	D	TA	SA1	22	B	TA	SA1	33	A	TA	SA2	44	B	TB	SB2

Topics & Subtopics

Code	Description	Code	Description
SA1	Instructional Leadership	SB2	Operational Management
SA2	Visionary Leadership	TA	Leadership
SB1	Organizational Management	TB	Management

CONTINUE ▶

TEST DIRECTION

Read the questions carefully and then choose the ONE best answer to each question.

Be sure to allocate your time carefully so you are able to complete the entire test within the testing session. You may go back and review your answers at any time.

You may use any available space in your test booklet for scratch work.

Questions in this booklet are not actual test questions but they are the samples for commonly asked questions.

This test aims to cover all topics which may appear on the actual test. However some topics may not be covered.

Studying this booklet will be preparing you for the actual test. It will not guarantee improving your test score but it will help you pass your exam on the first attempt.

Some useful tips for answering multiple choice questions;

- Start with the questions that you can easily answer.

- Underline the keywords in the question.

- Be sure to read all the choices given.

- Watch for keywords such as NOT, always, only, all, never, completely.

- Do not forget to answer every question.

1

Neurological disorders are diseases of the brain, spine and the nerves that connect them. There are more than 600 diseases of the nervous system, such as brain tumors, epilepsy, and Parkinson's disease. Which of the following neurological disorders may cause language delay?

A) Autism spectrum disorder
B) Developmental speech disorder
C) Cerebral palsy (CP)
D) All of the above

2

Which of the following term defines the measurement that shows the "average differences" from what most people score on a test?

A) Standard deviation
B) Mean
C) Median
D) Mode

3

A monthly "learning bulletin" has been developed in an elementary school where teachers provide the families of the students with information about what their children will be learning as well as what their respective families can do to aid in the child's learning at home. It includes tips for promoting students' homework completion and reinforcement strategies. Which of the following goals can be achieved with the help of learning bulletin?

A) Enlightening parents that teachers can best fulfill their responsibilities when families are willing to help.
B) Facilitating the ability of a teacher to address the required curriculum despite the constraints of available class time.
C) Prompting the families of the students to view themselves as people who can play a vital role in promoting the success of a student in school.
D) Ensuring personalized, motivating, and equitable learning opportunities for students who come from diverse backgrounds and different family situations.

4

Sweet spot enhances the ability to learn fast. What is the sweet spot for learning, when the task is neither too hard nor too easy?

A) The sweet zone
B) Zone of beginning
C) Zone of learning
D) Zone of the proximal development

5

Majority of the students of a specific school are non-English natives. According to a federal law, which of the following right do these students have?

A) Have their knowledge and skills be assessed in their most proficient language

B) Be provided with an educational setting with classmates of the same language

C) Be taught with the language that is comprehensible to them

D) Be taught with instructional materials that are written in their first language

6

Mrs. Ward's confusion on the school's next mission prompts her coworker to explain that the task is actually;

A) A financial report for all of the school's costs.

B) A general idea on the reaction of each member of the community.

C) A broad introduction on the way in which the school will achieve its vision.

D) An overall view of what the school plans to achieve.

7

Which of the following would most likely be the primary benefit of identifying and addressing gaps in a school's current math curriculum?

A) It would help teachers plan math instructions based on well-organized, and defined goals and objectives.

B) It would help facilitate the alignment between the instructions students receive and the learning materials they use in math.

C) It would help ensure appropriate instruction for students who have varying levels of math proficiency.

D) It would ensure that students would acquire the prerequisite math knowledge and skills that are needed to benefit from the following instruction.

During a classroom observation, a principal discovers that some teachers are inadvertently discriminating some of their students from particular groups by asking some students easier questions during class discussions or accepting work from some students that do not meet standards. Which of the following actions should the principal take that can best address this issue?

A) Suggest the use of self-reflection to help the teacher identify and analyze their problematic behaviors

B) Ask the teachers to describe their grading process as well as the criteria they use to evaluate the performance of the students in their class

C) Provide the teachers with concrete examples of the problematic patterns they are exhibiting

D) Review and discuss the anti-discrimination laws and policies to the teachers to help guide their interactions with their students

## 9

Which of the following is a supervisor most likely to do in a clinical supervision context?

A) Use a teacher's self-assessment of his or her needs to guide decisions about appropriate development experiences.

B) Create opportunities for a teacher to learn and grow in a collaborative team context.

C) Use observation and analysis to provide a teacher with feedback on aspects of performance needing improvement.

D) Focus on motivational or other personal issues that are affecting a teacher's effectiveness.

According to Perkins intelligence has three dimensions? Which of the following gives these components?

A) Reflective, Neural and Experiential

B) Neural, Experiential and Emotional

C) Neural, Emotional and Experiential

D) Emotional, Experiential and Reflective

Mr. Wilkins, a school principal, forms a staff committee to design a project that will improve student learning. Which of the following processes should Mr. Wilkins encourage the staff to do in developing the plan?

A) Design the project using the different perspectives reflected in the school's improvement plan.

B) Design the project using the recent students' assessment results.

C) Identify the possible impediments to the project and suggest solutions to overcome each.

D) Identify effective actions to solve school issues through data analysis.

12

A school where assessment is not currently used as a driving tool for instruction hires a new principal who has a goal of creating an effective, data-driven instructional program. Which of the following questions would be the most important one for the new principal to address first to achieve their goal?

A) What types of existing achievement issues at this school are best addressed through data analysis?

B) How can enough time for collaborative data analysis and discussion be built into teachers' schedules?

C) In determining when and how to use data analysis to plan instruction, how much flexibility should teachers have?

D) What is the most efficient way to involve a broad cross-section of school stakeholders in data analysis activities?

13

Mrs. Berckman, a fourth grade ENL teacher, has a newcomer student from a school in Honduras. It's the first time for the student to study in the U.S. Hence Mrs. Berckman finds it essential to assess the student's academic knowledge and skills.

What assessment should Mrs. Berckman use to yield the most useful information about the student's academic background?

A) An English proficiency test

B) An English norm-referenced battery of subject-area test

C) A Spanish proficiency test

D) A Spanish norm-referenced battery of subject-area test

14

Which of the following defines literacy skills?

A) It refers to the ways students interact with adults.

B) It is the ability to speak several languages.

C) It is the reasoning skills necessary to solve problems.

D) It is the knowledge and practices related reading and writing.

15

Which of the following is the purpose of instructional objectives?

A) To have the same ideas as the district's goals when it comes to student learning.

B) To have the school board develop teachers.

C) Applying teaching to students with various levels of ability.

D) To reflect each teacher's way of teaching.

16

What assessment measures a student's ability to learn in a specific situation?

A) CBM (Curriculum-Based Measure)

B) Diagnostic assessment

C) Dynamic assessment

D) An aptitude test

17

A principal calls a meeting to initiate changes that are aimed to improve teaching and learning in their school after seeing that their school performed poorly on state-mandated assessments. Which of the following ideas must the principal emphasize in the meeting to best promote the change?

A) The student test scores are only one among the many indicators of the quality of student learning that is happening at the school.

B) The individuals and groups within the educational community are sharing responsibility for the test results.

C) Statewide assessments are useful means to ensure educator accountability for student learning and achievement.

D) The test results can help the school staff identify and respond positively to specific problem areas by providing valuable information.

18

Which of the following questions about a lesson would most likely help a teacher grow professionally in his instructional practices?

A) How many students understood the material presented in the lesson by the end of the class period?

B) How did you respond to the disruption when several students entered the classroom late from another class?

C) What could you have done differently to help students succeed when they became confused during the lesson?

D) How well did students participate in the review exercises at the beginning of the lesson?

19

Which of the following changes in a learning environment is likely to have a positive effect on students' attitudes and motivation when it comes to learning?

A) Expanded use high-quality computer-based instruction

B) Focusing more on individual activities compared to group activities

C) Increased availability of adults who assist in the classroom

D) More instructional formats employed by the teacher

20

Most students who are English Language Learners (ELL) spend part of each day in ELL classes and part of the day in regular education classes. What can the school principal do to address the problem of the inability for the school to meet the current needs of English Language Learners ever since they've had a rapid increase in the proportion of students who are English Language Learners?

A) Increase the school's ELL staff by requesting funds and increasing the amount of time English Language Learners spend in ELL classes each day

B) Develop a system that would help teachers communicate with the administration about English Language Learners who are struggling in the classroom

C) Identify the teachers who need relevant professional development by surveying classroom teachers about their work with English Language Learners

D) Identify specific areas of needs by forming grade-level teacher teams who will analyze English Language Learners' classwork and test results

21

A new school introduced a school plan, which the teachers had willingly followed in its first year of implementation. This year, however, the school principal has noticed that a few teachers have departed from the original guidelines of the plan. How should the principal respond to this deviation?

A) Retrain those teachers who deviated from the original plan.

B) Evaluate the teachers' modifications whether they are effective in supporting the school's improvement plan.

C) Call the attention of the deviating teachers and stress to them the importance of consistent implementation.

D) Gather the teachers' views about the efficacy of the new plan.

22

Which of the following observations made by the principal is the best evidence that teachers are successfully applying the mastery learning model that they have learned about in professional development to improve student achievement?

A) Teachers collaborate with each other on a regular basis to plan lessons for the students in their classes who do not meet the curriculum standards on district and state assessments.

B) Department chairs in the school facilitate teacher discussion on weekly lesson planning sessions and encourage them to maintain rigor in classroom assessments.

C) Teachers start giving formative assessments during each study unit to measure the understanding of a student to determine if reteaching and retesting must be administered immediately.

D) Students who do not pass summative assessments will receive individualized instructional support from paraprofessionals in the classroom.

23

An effective teacher engages all students and provides a learning environment where all students can learn. Which of the following is a strategy used in effective teaching?

A) Breaking complex material down and making complicated topics easy to understand

B) Getting feedback from students and motivating them

C) Promoting student interest and giving plenty of examples to clarify the topic

D) All of the above

24

Principal's knowledge of the information is necessary to make instructional decisions. For determining strategies to improve third-grade students' achievement, which of the following information the principal needs?

A) The language arts standards for third-grade students and disaggregated standardized test data

B) The teachers' level of training and education of the third-grade teachers

C) The school's vision and mission

D) The number of newly enrolled students and the percentage rate of students who are still failing the exam

25

By considering which of the following first can the teacher prepare an effective lesson plan for a new instructional unit?

A) Unit activities best for individual and group work

B) The ways unit supports the goals of the district curriculum in the subject area

C) Background knowledge the students already have about the unit topic

D) The most efficient way to evaluate students' achievement of unit objectives

26

The curriculum is defined as the totality of student experiences that occur in the educational process. Which of the following about curriculum is not correct?

A) Curriculum planning is crucial because it makes classroom discipline easier.

B) A curriculum map is an ever-evolving document that should be followed based on the needs of the students.

C) Big ideas are essential in curriculum planning because it helps the teacher figure out what's most important about a curriculum.

D) Modern curriculum models are often a blend of process and product.

27

An elementary school and a community college start a tutoring program. Volunteer college students will be tutoring elementary school students who need extra help.

Which of the following teaching strategies will be the most effective for the tutors in supporting the elementary students' learning?

A) Supplying tutors with a detailed curriculum

B) Providing tutors with ongoing training and support

C) Requesting tutors to write a report after each class

D) Requesting tutors to write detailed lesson plans before each tutoring session

28

What was Eli M. Bower's contribution to the study of the education of children?

A) He was the first researcher to define high-functioning autism.

B) He conducted pioneering research on deficits in social imagination among children with Asperger's.

C) The discovery of autism and advocating for research on treatment options

D) Pioneering researcher on Cognitive Disorder.

29

School district supplies teachers with curriculum and necessary documents. Why should teachers still prepare annual and unit plans?

A) It is not necessary to develop annual and unit plans.

B) All school districts force teachers to write and submit annual and unit plans.

C) While preparing annual and unit plans by their own, teachers better understand what to teach.

D) Textbooks may not address all required standards, and teachers might have to supplement the curriculum.

30

Gestalt psychology is a movement in psychology founded in Germany in 1912, seeking to explain perceptions regarding gestalts rather than by analyzing their constituents and an attempt to understand the laws behind the ability to acquire and maintain meaningful judgments in a chaotic world.

Which of the following statements would be in agreement with Gestalt theory?

A) Single notes must remain constant to recognize an overall melody.

B) Pieces of a puzzle take priority over the total image.

C) Perceptual experience is more than the sum of its elements.

D) Slower the image projection faster the perception of movement.

31

Which of the following defines the role of a teacher in a student-centered environment?

A) Law enforcer who makes sure students are following the rules and regulations.

B) Co-teacher who works alongside the students to deliver lessons.

C) The organizer who monitors and supports student activities.

D) A dictator who tells students what to do and controls all their actions.

32

Which of the following about development is not correct?

A) B.F. Skinner has contributed to the behaviorist perspective of Educational Psychology.

B) Learning how to do addition is an example of cognitive development.

C) Environment influences a person's genes. This belief is an example of the interaction of DNA and heredity.

D) Emotional development is about understanding emotions while social development is about learning to interact with others.

33

Which of the following about intelligence and creativity development of a child is not correct?

A) The Theory of Multiple Intelligences was proposed by Gardner.

B) Intelligence remains stable, but IQ scores drop with age.

C) The Fagan test evaluates an infant's intelligence through her socio-motor skills.

D) IQ scores fluctuate during adolescence.

34

Backward Design is a method of designing educational curriculum by setting goals before choosing instructional methods and forms of assessment. In curriculum planning according to backward design principles, which one below is correct?

A) Design the end of the day before designing the beginning of the day.

B) Think of the big questions in a unit before the daily activities.

C) Start with plans for Friday and work backward to Monday.

D) Work on curriculum plans for June and move backward to September.

35

New programs will be implemented to address a school's problem on disparities in educational results among the student groups. However, many parents and community members express anger and dismay upon learning that the new programs will primarily be funded at the expense of existing school programs. How should the school principal respond to this protest?

A) Emphasize to everyone that it's a fair act to allow most significant support to the students' greatest academic weaknesses.

B) Emphasize to everyone that the entire community will reap significant benefits in the long run if all students are helped to succeed in school.

C) Explain to everyone that it's inevitable to compromise some priorities in times of financial stress.

D) Explain that school staff will maximize efficiency in delivering the new programs.

36

Which of the following terms mean thinking and learning about one's thinking processes?

A) Assimilation
B) Accommodation
C) Metacognition
D) Regulation of cognition

37

Using essay tests to evaluate student learning is an essential challenge for teachers. Which of the following is correct about the essay tests?

A) They are not useful in assessing specific kinds of thinking skills.

B) They tend to promote guessing in student answers.

C) Adjusting it to instructional objectives is hard.

D) It is hard to score them objectively and fair.

38

Which of the following does a raw score represent?

A) A family of scores that allow us to make comparisons between test scores.

B) Average performance at age and grade levels.

C) How close to the average the student's score fall.

D) The number of items a student answers correctly without adjustment for guessing.

39

Which of the following is the most effective method for obtaining an objective assessment of the success of a new language arts curriculum that will soon be implemented at a middle school by its educators?

A) Developing a plan for gathering data on student performance at selected points before and during the implementation

B) Collecting evidence of improvement since the implementation of the new curriculum by reviewing students' report cards at the end of the first marking term

C) Comparing state-mandated assessment scores of students from the previous year with the state-mandated assessment scores of students from the current year

D) Asking representative students and parent for their impressions of the effectiveness of the new program

40

Which of the following responsibilities is being fulfilled by a middle school principal when he/she decides to get the campus professional development to focus on finding ways to communicate high expectations to all students, regardless of gender, ethnicity, or disability?

A) Promoting the development of collegial relationships and teamwork between a diverse group of staff members

B) Establishing a collaboration between the staff for developing a shared vision of the school's mission

C) Ensuring that the campus is obeying all state and federal regulations

D) Helping shape a campus culture that responds to the diverse needs of the school community

41

When selecting reading materials to support the concepts presented in a lesson, a teacher should ask which of the following questions first?

A) Are these materials usable for more than one lesson presentation?

B) Will students require additional instruction to use these materials effectively?

C) Do these materials support a variety of student groupings?

D) Are these materials consistent with the students' comprehension and skill levels?

42

A teacher wishes to use scaffolding to boost student learning. Which of the following is the best example of this strategy?

A) Giving students charts labeled with relevant variables so that they can record data they gather during classroom science experiments

B) Prompting students to identify personal goals that they hope to achieve

C) Holding weekly geography bees with students to review relevant information covered during recent lessons

D) Marking errors in students' descriptive paragraphs and asking them to rewrite the sections correctly

43

If a student is interested in a subject, but the school does not offer any classes in it, in which way the student can acquire skills in this subject?

A) Reading books about the subject will enable the student to acquire desired skills.

B) He can not enroll in an outside course to learn because he is already enrolled in high school.

C) An internship or apprenticeship will provide instruction, modeling, and hands-on learning by doing.

D) He can find YouTube videos teaching the skills but not further reading/study matter.

Educational Psychology is the study of how humans learn and retain knowledge, primarily in educational settings like classrooms. It includes social, emotional and cognitive learning processes. Which of the following about Educational Psychology is not correct?

A) According to the Constructivist perspective the responsibility of learning falls on the learner rather than the teacher

B) Albert Bandura contributed a lot to the Social-Cognitive Educational Psychology.

C) Learning occurs through stage-like processes according to the Developmental Educational Psychology.

D) Learning occurs through observation according to the Cognitive Educational Psychology.

SECTION 4

#	Answer	Topic	Subtopic	#	Answer	Topic	Subtopic	#	Answer	Topic	Subtopic	#	Answer	Topic	Subtopic
1	D	TA	S1	12	B	TA	S1	23	D	TA	S1	34	B	TA	S1
2	A	TA	S1	13	D	TA	S1	24	A	TA	S1	35	B	TA	S2
3	C	TA	S1	14	D	TA	S1	25	C	TA	S1	36	C	TA	S1
4	D	TA	S1	15	A	TA	S1	26	A	TA	S1	37	D	TA	S1
5	C	TA	S1	16	C	TA	S1	27	B	TA	S2	38	D	TA	S1
6	C	TA	S1	17	A	TA	S1	28	B	TA	S1	39	A	TA	S1
7	D	TA	S1	18	C	TA	S1	29	D	TA	S1	40	D	TA	S2
8	C	TA	S1	19	A	TA	S1	30	C	TA	S1	41	D	TA	S1
9	C	TA	S1	20	D	TA	S1	31	C	TA	S1	42	A	TA	S1
10	A	TA	S2	21	B	TA	S1	32	C	TA	S1	43	A	TA	S2
11	D	TA	S1	22	C	TA	S1	33	C	TA	S2	44	D	TA	S1

Topics & Subtopics

Code	Description	Code	Description
SA1	Instructional Leadership	TA	Leadership
SA2	Visionary Leadership		

78

CONTINUE ▶

TEST DIRECTION

DIRECTIONS

Read the questions carefully and then choose the ONE best answer to each question.

Be sure to allocate your time carefully so you are able to complete the entire test within the testing session. You may go back and review your answers at any time.

You may use any available space in your test booklet for scratch work.

Questions in this booklet are not actual test questions but they are the samples for commonly asked questions.

This test aims to cover all topics which may appear on the actual test. However some topics may not be covered.

Studying this booklet will be preparing you for the actual test. It will not guarantee improving your test score but it will help you pass your exam on the first attempt.

Some useful tips for answering multiple choice questions;

- Start with the questions that you can easily answer.

- Underline the keywords in the question.

- Be sure to read all the choices given.

- Watch for keywords such as NOT, always, only, all, never, completely.

- Do not forget to answer every question.

CONTINUE ▶

1

Which of the following school practices should the principal be most concerned about after being informed by a superintendent that her primary goal must be to reduce the school's large achievement gap?

A) Allow teachers with poorly performing students to be rated "satisfactory" by using a teacher evaluation system

B) Base teacher hiring decisions more on previous classroom experience rather than on demographic background factors

C) Allow teachers to determine the school's professional development emphases for each school year through voting

D) Give teachers with the highest seniority and experience the priority to select courses they wish to teach

2

The principles of transparency are best illustrated in which situation below?

A) A due process procedure is strictly followed in disciplining an offensive student.

B) Reports on the status of school budget are regularly submitted to the superintendent.

C) A variety of stakeholders are recruited to create the vision and mission of the school.

D) Decisions in eliminating or adjusting school funding are justified with data and reasonable explanations.

3

Which of the following choices is the best approach a school principal must take to monitor routine custodial task?

A) Ask for a weekly summary of the previous week's activities from the head custodian

B) Conduct regular walk-throughs of the building using a checklist to note all the status of areas in that building

C) Advise teachers to contact the central office if classrooms and standard rooms are not properly maintained

D) Make unannounced inspections of different sections of the building and grounds in the early weeks of each school term

4

Which of the following strategies would be most useful for stakeholders to pursue first when wanting to develop a new vision of learning for an elementary school?

A) Using the visions of other district campuses as a model for their new vision

B) Conduct information gathering about the campus and community value

C) Aligning financial, human, and material resources behind the vision

D) Developing a collective plan to implement the new vision

Which of the following issues should the principal be most concerned about when performance on state assessments is used to enforce accountability in his school?

A) The substantial difference between the item formats used in most classroom tests and those used in state assessments

B) The inability of the school staff to access state assessments prior to test administration dates

C) The very limited opportunity given to students to do practice tests in preparation for the state assessments

D) The curriculum taught in the school not being closely aligned with the contents of the state assessments

## 6

One of the goals of an elementary school is to provide its students with equitable access to the curriculum. Which of the following should the school principal do to assess how well the school achieves this goal?

A) Ask the students what they have learned from the school so far.

B) Gather and evaluate various perspectives about the effectiveness and usefulness of curricular materials

C) Evaluate each component of the recent assessment results.

D) Determine the students' cultural profile.

## 7

Dropping out means leaving high school, college, university or another group for practical reasons, necessities, or disillusionment with the system from which the individual in question leaves.

Which of the following would help the principal to be aware of at-risk factors that lead students to drop out of high school?

A) Percent of low test scores

B) Low participation in school's extracurricular activities

C) Poor attendance

D) Class participation

The teacher instructs students to include drafts as well as final versions of the writing samples in their working portfolio. Which of the following is a primary benefit of using this type of portfolio with students?

A) It documents students' learning abilities over time.

B) It interprets one student's performance in relation to other students.

C) It provides a reliable means of predicting students' future performances.

D) It enables the teacher to determine students' mastery of large domains of content.

A school's budget will be reduced by 15 percent by mid-year. What should be the first step of the school principal to take in response to this problem?

A) Discuss with the school council which programs are most essential and thus should be retained.
B) Survey the students to determine the most valued school services.
C) Organize a fund-raising activity with the help of the school's stakeholders.
D) Revise the school budget plan for all programs, reducing the budget for each equally.

## 10

A computer is an electronic device that manipulates information or data. It can store, retrieve, and process data.

According to parents' survey, only a few of them have computers at home. For the principal to increase students' access to technology, which of the following should be his best approach for the school leadership to implement?

A) Extend the hours the school's computer labs are open to students.
B) Conduct fund-raising activities to provide families with computers.
C) Request more exclusive computers in the library that students without computers at home can use.
D) Do not give computer homework for students without computers at home.

"Dear Parents/Guardians,

Attached is an expenditure forecast document, per recent board decision regarding Pawnee School District's fiscal commitments going forward. This document is intended to familiarize district residents with expenditure projections which include nine major categories in our school budgets for the next five years.

Note that school budgets are driven by personnel costs which are then driven by student enrollment. Opportunely, increases in enrollment during the past years have subsided."

Given the draft letter above which is intended to inform parents and guardians about the district budget, how should it be edited so as to improve effectivity of the letter?

A) Replace costs with numerical values.
B) Use a more welcoming introduction.
C) Define technical terms.
D) Use simpler language and a less bureaucratic tone.

A principal wants to reverse the school trend toward declining writing scores on state assessment tests and decides that they would go about this by planning appropriate professional development activities for the school staff.

Which of the following would be the most efficient way to initiate this plan?

A) Determine writing skills that need improvement or subgroups of students that need additional support by examining previous data
B) Analyze publicly available information about the kinds of questions and tasks included in the state's writing assessment
C) Ask the teaching staff about their current teaching approaches when it comes to writing and how they incorporate writing into their classes
D) Seek information from the district language arts coordinator about high-quality resources available to enhance writing instruction

13

Which of the following would be the most likely outcome of significantly increasing the use of ability grouping for academic instruction within each classroom in an elementary school?

A) The curriculum will be taught more quickly and efficiently to students in each group by the teachers.

B) It will be more challenging for teachers to organize and implement data-driven differentiation and intervention.

C) The performance of the student will mostly meet the expectations based on the groups to which they are assigned to

D) The perception of the students to the learning environment overall will be more personalized and responsive to their strengths and needs

14

The goal of a low-performing elementary school is to significantly increase student performance in math and reading. The school's new principal decides to use large, brightly colored charts to display the changes in student performance in both math and reading over time. The charts will be displayed in a prominent spot in front of the cafeteria. What is the most significant benefit of the decision of the principal to use charts and tables?

A) It would provide a continuous reminder about the connection between daily learning activities and test performance to both students and staff

B) It makes critical information about the school readily available for inspection by all members of the school community

C) It would help communicate the school's commitment to improving student achievement to the entire school community

D) It enhances the recognition of both staff and students of the critical role of academic testing in the life of the school

15

Which of the following defines Sensory perception?

A) The awareness of things with the senses

B) The degree we respond to a stimulus

C) The level of strength of perception

D) The improvement in the sensation that is experienced with age

16

Cyberbullying has become a big issue at Arendale Middle School and to prevent further acts of violence, Mr. Anderson implemented a school safety plan. Assessments indicate a positive response from the students.

Which of the following should not be used to follow up on a safety plan?

A) Surveys

B) Routines

C) Meetings

D) Assessment

CONTINUE ▶

17

A web-based program of elective courses is being developed by collaborating high schools throughout the district. Selected teachers from each high school will provide online elective courses that any student attending any of the high schools in the district may be able to enroll to.

Which of the following is the greatest advantaged of the development of this kind of program?

A) The program maximizes curricular offerings in a cost-effective manner

B) The program standardizes the presentation of the instructional content across the district

C) The program would expose students to diverse peers and perspectives

D) The program would help promote a districtwide sense of accountability when it comes to teaching and learning

18

A principal decides to use a mentoring program after hiring a couple of new teachers. The mentoring program will pair a new teacher with a mentor teacher who has training roles arranged by the principal.

Which of the following actions should the principal take to ensure the success of the mentoring program?

A) Establish and maintain mentoring relationships between teachers by allocating time and resources to support the participants

B) Monitor progress and problems in the program by occasionally participating in meetings between the new teachers and their mentors

C) Provide the mentors with the educational and personal backgrounds of the teachers they will be mentoring

D) Obtain feedback from the new teachers on their mentors as well as the status of their mentoring relationships by planning regular meetings with them

## 19

In which of the following circumstances, a principal would be most justified in granting a teacher's request to remove a student from the classroom?

A) When the student's unwillingness to participate in group activities creates an unfair amount of work for other members of the groups where the student belongs to

B) When the student's unwillingness to complete assignments on time is negatively affecting the morale and motivation of other students

C) When the teacher determines that the student's behavior seriously interferes with the ability of the teacher to communicate effectively with other students

D) When the teacher determines that the student's classroom performance makes it highly unlikely that the student will be eligible for promotion

## 20

Mr. Hawkins, a newly-appointed principal, needs to create a new vision of his school to improve students' academic performance and boost the overall stakeholders' support for the school.

Which strategy would best ensure Mr. Hawkins that the new vision will have broad stakeholder support?

A) Presenting to the stakeholder's research-based values of school visions

B) Providing multiple opportunities for every stakeholder to participate in the visioning process

C) Presenting the school's current academic performance and its implication to the stakeholders

D) Creating a school committee to review the new vision and to suggest for revisions

21

Which of the following best describes the aesthetic associated with the regionalist movement?

A) Representing a view of the United States

B) Depicting the U.S. industrial machines

C) Celebrating the beauty of the U.S. landscape

D) Expressing the need for the United States to be more socially harmonious

22

To develop SMART goals, Mr. Mendel has to make his goals specific. How many "W" questions must he answer to do this?

A) 3

B) 4

C) 5

D) 6

23

The principal of a middle school has asked the district's gifted education coordinator to conduct periodic workshops to expand the teachers' knowledge and skills in providing instruction to academically gifted students assigned in their class.

Which of the following additional actions must a principal take to ensure best that the workshops will be a successful way of improving the teachers' performances in their respective classrooms?

A) Implement follow-up sessions that give teachers an opportunity to work together to evaluate and discuss their efforts at implementing new approaches

B) Arrange for a gifted education specialist to observe each teacher in the classroom after each workshop and report back to the administration on additional needs

C) Review plans for the workshops before they occur to ensure an emphasis on knowledge and procedures that have a foundation in current educational research

D) Provide teachers with a written summary of the main points addressed in each workshop and related ideas for improving their classroom instruction

24

Which of the following should the emphasis be included on during a pre-observation conference between a principal and a teacher in order to help promote an effective observation process?

A) Define the areas of performance that will be the primary focus for the observation

B) Review the teacher's prior observation results and determine their current relevance

C) Use a collaborative approach to design a checklist or other tools that the principal would use during the observation

D) Explore ways in which the lesson to be observed supports the school's vision, mission, and goals

25

Stacey, the school principal, held a meeting with the kindergarten teachers to discuss the transition from half-day to full-day kindergarten. The current teachers want to be part of the screening process for the new teachers. How should Stacey respond?

A) Allow the teachers to be part of the interview committee.

B) Choose the new teachers on your own.

C) Get suggestions from the current teachers, but do not let them conduct the interview.

D) Have the teachers she is closest to conduct the interview.

26

What is the most important advantage of a principal advising a new teacher to start making frequent use of various types of formative assessment in addition to the end-of-unit tests that they already use?

A) It gives a teacher a more data points for making grading decisions

B) It promotes a higher level of student motivation to master the content that is being taught

C) It allows the teacher to monitor the effectiveness of his or her instruction on an ongoing basis

D) It provides each student with more opportunities to become a successful learner

27

A walkthrough is a step-by-step test of all aspects of an environment, plan, or process to verify if it is ready for its intended purpose.

Which of the following should principal do to help teachers accept change for the new plans of implementing walkthroughs as part of the teacher evaluation process?

A) Ask teachers' colleagues to convince others

B) Tell the teachers about the benefits of having walkthrough based on the principal's experience

C) Assign professional to explain the details of the new plan to the teachers

D) Provide teachers with opportunities to research the benefits of walk-throughs as part of the evaluation process

After the completion of three hands-on workshops on instructional strategies for meeting the needs of students who have learning disabilities, which of the following steps the Principal must take so that there will be an increase in the achievement for the targeted student population?

A) Create teacher teams that would give time for team members to observe and coach one another on the use of the strategies they've learned.

B) Require teachers to debrief the principal on the strategies they are using and their respective effects on the students with learning disabilities.

C) Supplement information provided in the workshops with professional articles on practical applications of the strategies.

D) Have a Special Education staff in the school or district send teachers a weekly e-mail that includes easy-to-implement tips for using the strategies.

The mission of the School Improvement Planning and Internal Audit Division is to provide efficient procedures for the Jones County Schools.

What is an internal audit?

A) A way to avoid accountability

B) A compulsory contracted agreement

C) A method to evaluate the finances and risks

D) A process to report school demographic process

30

Mr. Russel, a tenured teacher, had not been satisfactorily performing his job. One of the building leaders noticed this and asked the school district leader to support him in initiating proceedings to terminate Mr. Russel. Which of the following should the district leader have before agreeing to help the building leader?

A) Proof of Mr. Russel's actions that conflict with the district code of conduct

B) Test scores that prove Mr. Russel's incompetence

C) Student evaluation sheets

D) A record of actions taken to settle Mr. Russel's weaknesses

31

Ms. Agdaca is the leader of a district's Shared-Decision-Making Team. She feels that the team has not been functioning as efficiently as it should. She asked the team members to evaluate themselves through a questionnaire. What should be the next step?

A) The team discusses the results of the evaluation and plan on how to improve on their weaknesses.

B) The team leader analyzes the results of the evaluation and instructs the team how to proceed.

C) The team leader talks to each member privately to discuss what his/her part should be in improving team functioning.

D) The team leader assigns a member to organize an open forum.

32

Performance standards are expectations for instruction, assessment, and student work while content standards define the knowledge within each discipline.

Which of the following is the difference between performance and content standards?

A) Performance standards allow critical thinking for students.

B) Performance standards are different from each grade levels.

C) Performance standards measure student competency against content standards.

D) Performance standards measure students' competitiveness with each other.

33

Spencer is the principal of a traditionally small and homogenous elementary school. In the past five years, there has been an influx of immigrants in her school. How should she start addressing this new need?

A) Ask teachers for suggestions regarding new programs

B) Review current programs

C) Make sure that ESOL programs follow state and federal guidelines

D) Survey where the highest number of immigrants come from and let this serve as a basis for new programs

34

Asperger Syndrome (AS) is a neurobiological disorder on the higher-functioning end of the autism spectrum.

Which of the following is characteristic of a child with Asperger's Syndrome?

A) The difficulty with social interactions such as speaking and forming complete sentences.

B) High academic performance and cognitive development.

C) Inability to acquire new information in classes such as mathematics.

D) Delayed mental development and motor skills development.

35

Mr. Swanson, a school district leader, is managing the planning for the enhancement the use of classroom assessment. This aims to improve student learning outcomes.

What provisions should the plan include so that it would achieve its intended goal?

A) Enforcing that students be evaluated on standardized assessment practices and grading criteria

B) Ensuring that students are allowed to have options to demonstrate their intelligence

C) Ensuring that assessment is considered as the primary tool for making instructional decisions

D) Establishing individualized tests for slow learners

36

A principal wants to reiterate the benefits of family-community involvement in school improvement efforts. Research shows that students tend to earn higher grades, attend school more regularly, stay in school longer, and enroll in higher-level programs.

Which of the following is the significant benefit parent, family and community involvement in educational improvement?

A) Form partnerships that foster higher educational aspirations and more motivated students.

B) Inform parents and community members more on the school's rules and regulations.

C) Collect the higher amount of funds for school projects and developments.

D) Give more information on parents on how to handle their children.

37

Which of the following would help the principal to determine the most important consideration when community resources are integrated into classroom instruction?

A) Can the resources be used to their maximum?

B) Are the resources easy to manage?

C) Can the resources be used simultaneously?

D) Do the resources meet the needs of the program?

38

What action should a school building leader take to promote the faculty and staff's professional development?

A) Encouraging teachers to participate in development programs

B) Requiring teachers to attend development programs

C) Giving demerits to teachers who fail to participate in development programs

D) Making professional development criteria for evaluation of teachers

94

CONTINUE ▶

## 39

A school principal is committed to ensuring effective and equitable learning opportunities for all students. In what way can the principal best demonstrate his commitment?

A) Encouraging teachers to use individualized standards for guiding instructional practices

B) Distributing the school's financial resources in proportion to its number of students

C) Making decisions about students' concerns by integrating various factors

D) Encouraging the implementation of differentiated instructions to meet the students' diverse needs

## 40

A teacher asks students to predict the outcome of a story and tells their partners their predictions after one minute and have some of them described to the class.

Which of the following did the students make use of during this activity?

A) Reciprocal teaching

B) Think-pair-share

C) Shared reading

D) Anticipation guide

SECTION 5

#	Answer	Topic	Subtopic	#	Answer	Topic	Subtopic	#	Answer	Topic	Subtopic	#	Answer	Topic	Subtopic
1	D	TB	SB1	11	D	TB	SB2	21	B	TA	SA2	31	A	TB	SB1
2	D	TB	SB1	12	A	TA	SA1	22	D	TB	SB1	32	C	TA	SA1
3	B	TB	SB2	13	C	TA	SA1	23	A	TA	SA1	33	C	TA	SA2
4	B	TA	SA2	14	C	TA	SA2	24	A	TA	SA1	34	A	TA	SA1
5	D	TA	SA1	15	A	TA	SA1	25	A	TB	SB2	35	C	TA	SA1
6	C	TA	SA1	16	B	TB	SB2	26	C	TA	SA1	36	A	TB	SB1
7	C	TA	SA1	17	A	TA	SA1	27	D	TA	SA1	37	D	TA	SA1
8	A	TA	SA1	18	A	TB	SB2	28	A	TA	SA1	38	D	TB	SB1
9	A	TB	SB2	19	C	TA	SA2	29	C	TB	SB1	39	D	TA	SA1
10	A	TA	SA2	20	B	TA	SA2	30	D	TB	SB2	40	D	TA	SA1

Topics & Subtopics

Code	Description	Code	Description
SA1	Instructional Leadership	SB2	Operational Management
SA2	Visionary Leadership	TA	Leadership
SB1	Organizational Management	TB	Management

CONTINUE ▶

Made in United States
North Haven, CT
14 February 2022

16101304R00059